YORKSHIRE
— THE LIGHT AND THE LAND —
PHOTOGRAPHS BY COLIN BAXTER

DAVID & CHARLES

Newton Abbot   London

British Library Cataloguing in Publication Data

Baxter, Colin
  Yorkshire: the light and the land.
  I. Title
  914.28'104858

  ISBN 0-7153-9164-X h/bk
  ISBN 0-7153-9386-3 p/bk

First published 1989
Second impression 1989

Printed in Italy
by New Interlitho S.p.A., Milan
for David & Charles Publishers plc
Brunel House   Newton Abbot   Devon

INTRODUCTION

Yorkshire to me is the memory of what it felt like to be in the many special situations recorded in this book.

Cycling along the tracks high above Farndale and Rosedale in the North Yorkshire Moors on a cold December day, the light low and warm despite my slightly numb fingers. A streamer of smoke from heather burning fans out to cloak the scooped-out dale with a veil of strange oranges.

Standing high above Swaledale on a June evening with sun streaming on the vivid green fields and giant jigsaw patterns of infamous dry stone walls, wondering at the freshness of the wind, the space to breathe, and how the encroaching front of cloud looks so mauve, not grey at all.

It has just stopped teeming rain on Scarborough harbour one November afternoon, the dark sky producing a premature twilight. There is that perfect balance between daylight and the artificial lights that have been switched on. I seem to be able to smell the fishing boat a couple of hundred yards away, and my eyes home in on a photograph. The grand whitewashed hotel terraces stand high across the bay and harbour, looming in the pink half-light.

You cannot fail to notice what must be one of Britain's largest power stations huddled in a corner where the M62 and A1 meet. One day, travelling south, as the sun sets in my mirror, I watch the steam belch furiously out of all eight cooling towers, and wonder excitedly what this monstrosity of power looks like back-lit. So we turn north and find a point just off the road, (in sticky mud, I remember), to witness the most beautiful effect of light, steam and giant man-made shapes.

At the end of May, in Wharfedale, we decide to explore Malham. Approaching from above, we walk down the steep road and then, over a stile set into a stone wall, there is a perfect vista of the cove, dropping abruptly down to the well-trodden path. We sit for a while and watch the shadows of fluffy clouds drift across that spectacle of rural construction, those limestone walls wriggling round the sheep. I snatch rectangles from their design, (the front cover), feeling a mixture of privilege and guilt to watch at leisure the enduring result of such immense labour.

It is so heartening to come across stone building work still being carried out on new buildings. Many places in Britain could learn a great deal from the planning and agricultural control of rural Yorkshire. For it is not just light and land which combine to make these special situations: man's own mark on the landscape is almost always visible, and if that mark is made sensibly, and in some harmony with the surroundings, then the beauty of the landscape can even be enhanced. Swaledale without walls and barns is hard to imagine: in fact, I'd rather not even imagine it. I would prefer to savour the memory of being there, the feeling of looking at such natural and man-made beauty, and the thought of returning to this intriguingly diverse county.

Colin Baxter 1989

ADDLEBROUGH AND ASKRIGG

INGLEBOROUGH

BOONHILL COMMON

GREENCLIFFE HAG WOOD

HAWORTH

SUN SIDE, SWALEDALE

HAGG COMMON

ROBIN HOOD'S BAY FROM SOUTH CHEEK

ROBIN HOOD'S BAY – THE VILLAGE

NR. STARBOTTON

YEW COGAR SCAR

LOW ROW PASTURE

COCKAYNE RIDGE

ROULSTON SCAR

WALLS OF STONE

THWAITE SIDE

POCKLEY MOOR

HIGH BLAKEY MOOR

HUTTON BECK

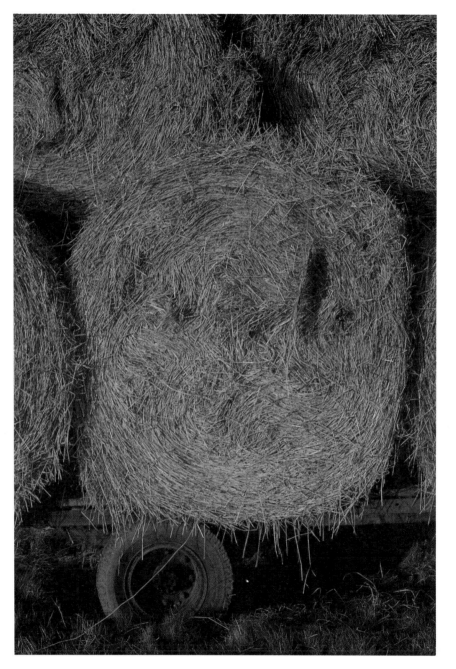

OLD BYLAND

OUGHTERSHAW SIDE

CAM FELL AND INGLEBOROUGH

BAGBY

FERRYBRIDGE POWER STATION

BOOTHAM BAR AND YORK MINSTER

THE SHAMBLES, YORK

DOORWAY, YORK

GROAT HILL, BRANSDALE

SUMMER LODGE MOOR

ROMBALDS MOOR

OLD COTE MOOR

ASHBERRY FARM, RIEVAULX

AGGLETHORPE, COVERDALE

HALIFAX

40

CHISERLEY

WESTERDALE MOOR

ELBOLTON, WHARFEDALE

HAWORTH AT DUSK

SLEDDALE BECK

RUDLAND RIGG

CRACKPOT SIDE AND SWALEDALE

HUTTON-LE-HOLE

FARNDALE

RIEVAULX ABBEY

NR. HELMSLEY

FYLINGDALES MOOR

DOORWAYS, WHITBY

RIVER WHARFE

KIRK GILL MOOR

GUNNERSIDE

THE LIGHT

SMARBER, SWALEDALE

COVERDALE

TERRACED HOUSE

HEBDEN BRIDGE

GREAT SLED DALE

BRIMHAM ROCKS

UPPER WHARFEDALE

GRASSINGTON

STAITHES

WHITBY ABBEY

WHITBY AT DUSK

CHURCH STREET, WHITBY

ARNCLIFFE

HIGH BERGH, LITTONDALE

STOODLEY PIKE

RAYDALE

LEVISHAM MOOR

WENSLEYDALE

GREAT FRYUP DALE   NR. KETTLEWELL, WHARFEDALE

HOW STEAN BECK

HORSE HEAD MOOR

DOUTHWAITE DALE

LANGSTROTHDALE

RYE DALE

LINTON

FOUNTAINS FELL

DODD FELL

EAST COAST CLIFFS

SCARBOROUGH HARBOUR

BISHOPSIDE, NIDDERDALE

HELMSLEY CASTLE

STOUPE BROW

HEPTONSTALL

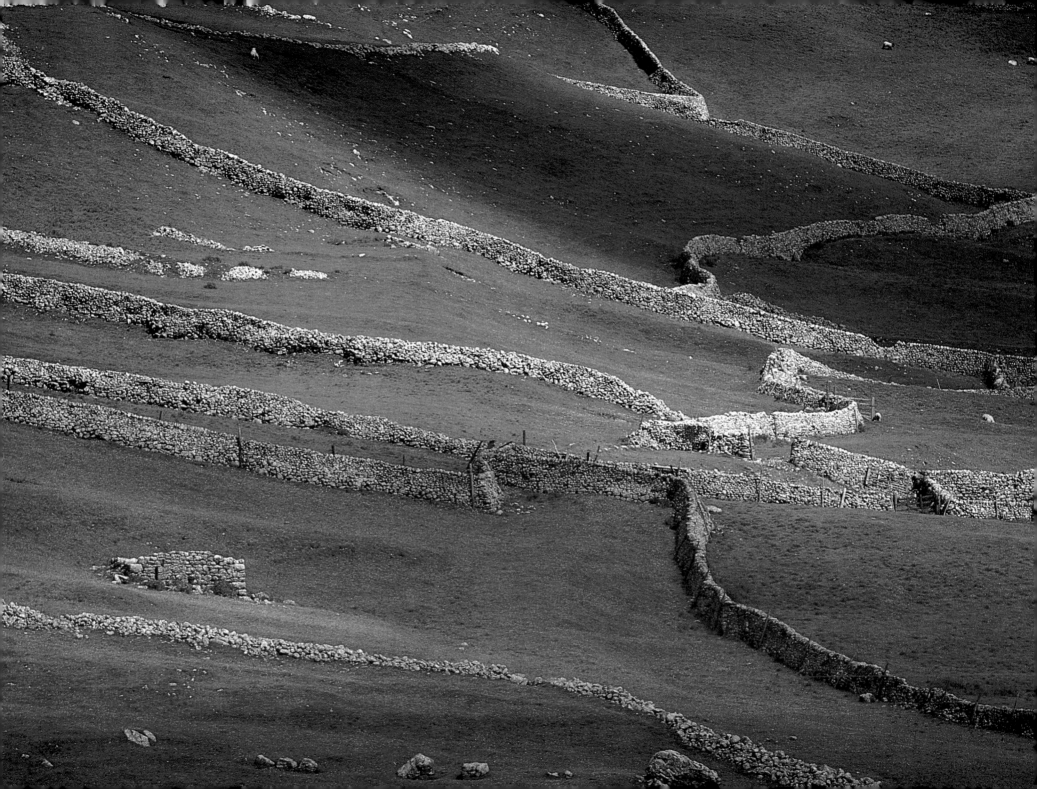

SHORKLEY HILL

BEADLAM RIGG

BISHOP THORNTON

HIGH PASTURE

INDEX